THE
GAMES
BOOK

Written by Huw Davies
Illustrated by Lisa Jackson

THE
GAMES
BOOK

SCHOLASTIC INC.

NEW YORK   TORONTO   LONDON   AUCKLAND   SYDNEY
MEXICO CITY   NEW DELHI   HONG KONG   BUENOS AIRES

The publisher and authors disclaim, as far
as is legally permissible, all liability for accidents,
injuries, or loss that may occur as a result of the
information or instructions given in this book.

Exercise good common sense at all times; stay within
the law and rules and be considerate of other people.

No part of this publication may be reproduced, stored in a retrieval system, or
transmitted in any form or by any means, electronic, mechanical, photocopying,
recording, or otherwise, without written permission of the publisher. For information
regarding permission, write to Michael O'Mara Books Limited, 9 Lion Yard, Tremadoc
Road, London, SW4 7NQ, United Kingdom.

Library of Congress Cataloging-in-Publication data is available.

ISBN-13: 978-0-545-13403-3
ISBN-10: 0-545-13403-X

First published in Great Britain in 2008
by Michael O'Mara Books Limited,
9 Lion Yard, Tremadoc Road, London, SW4 7NQ, United Kingdom.
www.mombooks.com

Copyright © 2008 Michael O'Mara Books Limited

Cover design by Zoe Quayle
Cover image by Paul Moran

12 11 10 9 8 7 6 5 4 3 2 1   9 10 11 12 13 14/0

Printed in the U.S.A.
First American edition, August 2009

CONTENTS

Introduction

The games described in this book will take you back in time, to an era in which children's television wasn't available morning, noon, and night; there was no such thing as a computer game; and the Internet wasn't even a glimmer in its creator's eye.

This was a wild, lawless time, when children ran around in fields on long summer evenings — hiding and seeking, chasing and catching, staying out past dinnertime, bedtime even.

We hope this book will spark lots of happy memories, and also rekindle enthusiasm for all the games in danger of being drowned beneath the tide of the digital age.

Deciders

Before any game can begin, there are decisions to be made.
Whether you need to choose who will be It or who starts a
game, keep things fair using one of these "deciders."

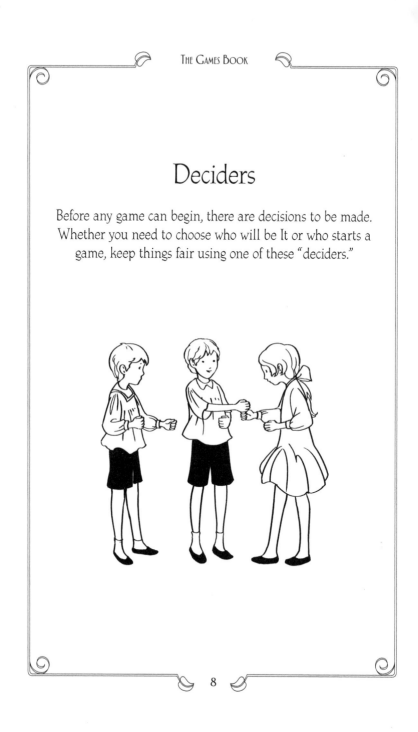

Dips

Dipping is a perfect way to eliminate arguments over who goes first. It uses a rhyme as a process of elimination and is a pleasantly long-winded game in itself.

Gather everyone who wants to play and, while reciting a rhyme, count around the group, one person per word. The person counted on the last word is eliminated.

Repeat the process until all but one is out, leaving that player to start the game. Here are a few rhymes to get you started:

> *Dip, dip, dip,*
> *My blue ship,*
> *Sailing on the water,*
> *Like a cup and saucer,*
> *Dip, dip, dip,*
> *You aren't It.*

Ip dip, sky blue,
Who's It? Not you.
Not because you're dirty,
Not because you're clean,
But because my mother says
You're the Fairy Queen.

Eeny, meeny, miny, moe,
Catch a tiger by the toe,
If he hollers, let him go,
Eeny, meeny, miny, moe.

Two, four, six, eight,
Mary's at the cottage gate,
Eating cherries off a plate,
Two, four, six, eight.

Each peach, pear, plum,
Out goes Tom Thumb.
Tom Thumb won't do,
Out goes Betty Blue.
Betty Blue won't go,
So out goes you.

Spuds

If everyone is fighting over who goes first, shout "Spuds out!" Everyone then gathers in a circle, hands held out in fists, or "spuds."

Walk around the circle knocking on each spud with your fist, reciting as you go:

> One potato, two potato,
> Three potato, four,
> Five potato, six potato,
> Seven potato, MORE!

The spud knocked on "MORE" goes behind the player's back, and the count continues until all spuds but one are eliminated. The owner of that spud is It.

Remember to include your own spuds in the count, knocking each fist on top of the other. If you are down to just one spud, count by knocking it gently against your chin.

Rock, Paper, Scissors

Rock, Paper, Scissors is a great way of deciding who goes first or who is It. It's also a very entertaining game. All you need are your hands, sharp wits, and a worthy opponent.

How to Play

Facing each other, two players hold out a fist and use it to beat out the rhythm while chanting, "Rock, Paper, Scissors." Then each player shows one of these three shapes:

Rock: A clenched fist.
Paper: The hand opened out flat.
Scissors: The first two fingers extended.

The aim is to choose a shape that beats your opponent's.

Paper beats rock because paper can wrap around a rock.
Rock beats scissors because scissors can't cut a rock.
Scissors beats paper because scissors can cut paper.

If you both choose the same shape, it's a tie, and you must try again.

Play a single game if you need a quick decision, or "best of three" or "best of five."

Tactical Tip

Cheating is possible — a player can delay making a shape until the moment after the opponent has shown his or her shape. Deal with cheaters by having players make the shape behind their backs, then show them at the same time.

Party Games

This selection of party classics will keep your guests busy for hours and will help make any child's party a huge success.

Blind Man's Bluff

A party favorite, Blind Man's Bluff has been played for hundreds of years. It works well with at least six players, depending on the size of the room you are playing in. This game is sure to wear out even the most energetic guests.

How to Play

In the classic version of Blind Man's Bluff, one person is blindfolded and spun around three times by the other players until that person is disoriented. The Blind Man then moves around the room, with hands outstretched, and attempts to tag the other players. The other players run around the room keeping out of the Blind Man's reach as long as possible. The last person to be tagged is the winner.

Variations

Players can remain stationary, either seated or standing, while the Blind Man seeks them out. They are allowed to bend and twist out of reach, but they cannot actually move from their spot.

In another version, the Blind Man has to try to guess who is in their grasp. They can use their hands to feel the person's features. If they succeed they can hand over the blindfold, but if they fail they must continue trying to tag another player.

Tactical Tips

If you are the Blind Man, remember to use your other senses to help you hunt players down. The sound of someone giggling or a waft of air as someone brushes past you will help enormously.

Whichever version of the game you decide to play, it's best to keep doors shut and clear the room of any clutter before you start, to avoid injuring the Blind Man.

Hotter, Colder

Perfect for a traditional party, Hotter, Colder is a hiding and hunting game that is played indoors.

How to Play

Select a small household object — anything from a pencil to a button is perfect. One player, the Hunter, leaves the room for a minute, while the other players decide on a hiding place for the chosen object.

The Hunter is allowed back into the room and starts to search for the object. The only clues the other players can give are "Hotter" the nearer the Hunter gets to the object, or "Colder" if the Hunter moves away from it. If the Hunter gets very close, they can shout "Burning," and if the Hunter is completely off course, they can shout "Freezing."

When the object is found, another player leaves the room and the object is hidden again.

The difficulty of this game depends on the size of the object hunted and the area in which it's hidden — this can be varied according to the age and ability of the players.

If the object is too small and difficult to find, or if there are too many obscure hiding places, the game can go on for ages, so you may want to put a time limit on searches.

Reverse Rule

A variation of this game is to have many Hunters. One player hides the object while all the others are out of the room. When the Hunters return, they are directed with a shout of "Hotter" or "Colder" until someone succeeds in finding it.

Wink Murder

Wink Murder is a game of cunning and trickery. It requires a minimum of five players, and is perfect to play around the dinner table.

How to Play

Tear off a piece of paper for each person. Mark one with an *X* and leave the rest blank. Scrunch each of them up into a ball and place them in a hat or bowl.

Pass the hat around for each player to take a paper ball. Players must open their paper balls discreetly. One person will find he or she has the paper with the *X,* and this means he or she will play the part of the Murderer. Everyone else is both a potential victim and a detective.

The aim for the Murderer is to "kill" all the players around the table without getting caught. To kill someone, the Murderer must catch his or her eye and subtly wink at him or her without the other players noticing.

The aim for the other players is to identify the Murderer before they become victims.

The game begins, and everyone around the table must look at one another in turn, making eye contact. When the Murderer strikes, his or her victims use their acting skills as they keel over and die dramatic deaths.

Anyone who thinks they have figured out who the Murderer is can formally accuse him or her. But if that person is incorrect, the punishment is death!

A variation can be played with a designated Detective who sits among the murder victims. If the Detective successfully identifies the killer before everyone is dead, the Murderer becomes the next Detective. If not, that person remains Detective for the next game.

Tactical Tip

If you are the Murderer, take your time choosing your victims. Don't begin with the people directly opposite you, since that will make you a prime suspect.

Sleeping Lions

Perfect for any moment when noise and excitement levels have reached a peak, Sleeping Lions is a parental party favorite. Simply get all the players to lie on their backs on the floor and compete to be the stillest, quietest Lion of all.

If asked to keep their eyes shut, some may even fall asleep.

Now, tiptoe away and start cleaning up.

Charades

This classic play-acting game is great fun at family gatherings, when a normally serious aunt or uncle can have everyone in stitches. A minimum of four players is required.

How to Play

Divide into two teams and give each team a bowl and a pencil and paper.

Out of your opponents' earshot, choose a selection of titles from TV shows, movies, plays, books, musicals, or songs. Well-known phrases or famous quotations are also allowed. Write each title down on a separate scrap of paper, fold them all up, and place them in your bowl.

Select a team to go first and a member of that team to be the first mime artist. The mime artist picks a title from the other team's bowl and silently reads it. The player's task is to communicate the title picked to the rest of their team using nothing but mime. No props or noises are allowed.

A time limit is agreed on for each turn (two minutes is standard), and a timer or watch is used to enforce the limit.

Mime Time

If you are the mime artist, start by describing the type of title you have picked. Here are the established mimes for each genre:

Song: Cup hands around open mouth to indicate singing a song.

Movie: Pretend to crank an old-fashioned movie camera.

Play: Draw both hands apart, as if opening stage curtains.

Book: Palms together, open them up like a book.

Television show: Draw a rectangle in the air with your fingers.

Phrase or quotation: Use index fingers to draw quotation marks in the air.

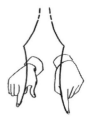

Musical: Go down on one knee with one arm held out dramatically.

Word Count

Next, show how many words are in the title by holding up the correct number of fingers. Alternatively, you can sweep your arms in a wide circle to show you are going to act out the whole thing without breaking it into individual words.

If you break the title into individual words, you hold up your fingers to specify which word you will be attempting. You can even break a word up into syllables to make it easier to guess. To show the number of syllables in a word, hold the

appropriate number of fingers against one forearm, then do the same to indicate which of the syllables you are miming first.

For any small words in the title, such as *a, it,* or *of,* you should hold a thumb and forefinger close together to show a small size.

If a word is difficult to convey, but an easier word sounds similar, a tug of the earlobe indicates "sounds like."

Getting It Right

When a member of your team guesses a word accurately, you tap your nose and point straight at the person who guessed correctly.

If the whole title is guessed in time, your team wins a point. If your team runs out of time, or only guesses part of the title, you do not score. In both cases, play passes to the opposing team.

Tactical Tip

Be sure the titles you write down for the opposing team are as difficult to mime as possible.

Musical Chairs

This classic party game is usually played by children, but sometimes grown-ups can't resist joining in. You will need several chairs — one fewer than there are participants — and a source of music, such as a CD player or piano.

How to Play

The chairs are arranged in two columns, back-to-back with the seats facing out. One person is in charge of the music.

When the music starts, everyone walks, or dances, in a line around the chairs. The musical controller or pianist stops the music at random, and everyone must sit down as quickly as possible, leaving one person without a chair.

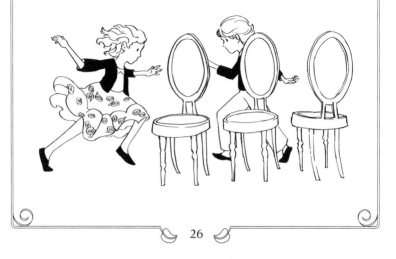

That person is out of the game. A chair is removed, and the game begins again.

In each round the last player to reach a chair is out, until there is just one player left. That person is the winner.

Variation

If space allows, a good alternative is to arrange the chairs in a circle or a square, with one chair per person. Everyone dances in a line, moving clockwise around the chairs.

In this version, all players must remember their original chairs. When the music stops, everyone races back to his or her own chair by continuing in a clockwise direction. The last person to sit down is eliminated, and that chair is taken away.

Simon Says

Simon Says is a timeless party game that can be played with large or small numbers of people.

How to Play

Decide which person will be Simon. Simon stands in front of the other players and tells them to perform certain actions, such as jumping in the air, touching their noses, turning around, wiggling their fingers, shouting "Hello!," and so on. The actions can be anything Simon thinks of, as long as everyone playing is capable of doing them.

The key to the game is whether or not Simon adds the words "Simon says" before an instruction.

If Simon says, "Simon says wiggle your fingers," then everyone must wiggle their fingers. If Simon just says "Wiggle your fingers," no one must wiggle their fingers. If you do not perform the command or if you do it incorrectly, you're out.

The last player left wins. The winner can be presented with a prize or he or she can play the part of Simon in the next round.

Tactical Tips

Simon can trick players into making mistakes. He could say, "Simon says raise your left arm," while raising his right arm. Alternatively, he could disguise a command. For example, he can say, "Can someone go and see if Mom's in the living room?"

Statues

A game of balance and control, Statues challenges everyone's ability to think quickly and keep their balance.

How to Play

For the simplest game of Statues, a player is chosen to be It and the rest become human statues.

To start, It turns away. The statues then run, jump, prance, and dance around as much as they like. However, It can turn around at any time, and all the statues must freeze immediately in whatever position they find themselves at that moment.

It can walk around among the statues to be sure that no one moves a muscle. Anyone who does is out of the game.

To restart play, It shouts "Go" and turns away again. The winner is the last person to be caught moving.

Musical Statues

To turn Statues into Musical Statues, simply add music. The person chosen to be It gets to control the music.

The statues dance around until It suddenly stops the music. The players must then come to a complete standstill. Any player caught moving is out. Then the music resumes, and the last person standing is the winner.

Musical Bumps

Musical Bumps is an ideal alternative for more active competitors who don't mind falling to the floor.

Instead of having to freeze in an awkward position when the music stops, players must sit down on the ground as quickly as they can.

The last player to sit down is out.

Playground Games

Recess has never been so much fun! These games are
great to play in large, open spaces.

Red Rover

Red Rover is a game of strength played between two teams.

How to Play

Divide into two teams. One is the "chain" and links hands, facing the other team about 12 feet away. The chain team challenges a member of the other team by chanting:

Red Rover, Red Rover,
We call [David] over!

David charges at the chain, trying to break through. If he succeeds, his team can pick a player from the chain to join their team. If he fails, he has to join the chain. The winner is the last person who is free.

Tactical Tip

Challenge smaller players. They are unlikely to break through your chain and will be obliged to join your team.

Sly Fox

Any number of players can join in this playground favorite as long as you have enough open space. One child acts as Grandmother, while the rest act like sly foxes trying to sneak up behind her, hoping to reach her before she can see them moving.

How to Play

Select a player to be Grandmother, then stand in a line, about 10 feet behind her. As soon as she turns her back to the other players, they must start trying to creep up on her and touch her on the shoulder.

Grandmother can turn around at any time without warning, and players must freeze instantly. If she sees anyone moving, they are sent back to the starting point. The first person to tap her on the shoulder becomes Grandmother.

To give the players enough time to get moving, Grandmother must count to ten quietly. There is no restriction on the speed at which she counts, so watch out!

Tactical Tips

Your triumph will depend more on the strategy you choose, plus a bit of luck, than your speed and strength. Inching forward, as slowly as possible, means that you'll be much harder to catch, but you'll take a long time to get anywhere near Grandmother. Rushing to cover as much ground as you can is risky because you may not be able to stop quickly enough when she suddenly turns around. Either way, it's important to keep a close eye on Grandmother for any signs that she might spin around.

Follow the Leader

At its most extreme, this game can become a march across fields and woods, with the Leader challenging followers with a variety of actions. At its most basic, it is a simple party game that all small children can enjoy.

How to Play

Choose one player to be the Leader. Often this will be the boy or girl with the most energy, or the person everyone else thinks is the most adventurous.

The Leader begins walking with all the other players in a line behind him or her. The Leader can go anywhere and carry out any actions — a whistle, a shout, a jump, a cartwheel, a funny

dance, and so on — and the followers must copy exactly. If they don't, they are out of the game.

The Leader must test the abilities of the followers as much as possible. This is what makes the game fun, but be sure to avoid anything that's truly dangerous.

The game continues until all the followers refuse to do something, give up, and drop out. If the Leader starts to get tired, a replacement can step in at any time.

What Time Is It, Mr. Fox?

A simple yet suspenseful game of chase that is always extremely popular with children, What Time Is It, Mr. Fox? can be played almost anywhere, as long as there is a reasonable amount of space to walk and run in.

How to Play

Choose a starting point that will also be the "safe" area to return to when the chase is on. Mr. Fox is selected and walks away from the rest of the players in a straight line, while they follow.

The followers regularly call out, "What time is it, Mr. Fox?" and Mr. Fox replies by saying, "Nine o'clock," "Five o'clock," or any other randomly chosen time.

Each time the followers ask, "What time is it, Mr. Fox?" they should dare themselves to get nearer. Mr. Fox will be able to tell by the sound of their voices how close they might be. When he thinks he might be able to catch one of them, he'll wait to be asked the time again, then turn unexpectedly, growling, "Dinnertime!" Then he'll chase everyone back to the safe area. Whoever is caught becomes the next Mr. Fox.

Tactical Tips

If you are following Mr. Fox, try not to give away your location by shouting out the question any louder than the other players. Also, noisy feet will alert Mr. Fox to your location very quickly.

Adder's Nest

Adder's Nest is an old game that is a great test of strength
and guile — all you need is a central object to represent
a nest, such as a drain or manhole cover. Oh, and strong arms
are a must.

How to Play

Players make a circle of five or six people around the nest.
Each player holds hands with the people on either side of
him or her. The circle gathers as close to the nest as possible
and chants:

> *Five little sausages frying in a pan,*
> *One went pop and the others went BANG!*

On "BANG!" everyone jumps back from the nest and the
battle begins, as players attempt to pull one another onto
the nest and keep themselves as far from it as possible.

Anyone who touches the nest is "poisoned" and out of the
game, but this counts only if the circle was not broken at
the time.

The game continues with a smaller circle each time until just two players remain, fighting it out to be the winner.

Tactical Tip

If a player next to you seems particularly strong, try to outwit him or her by allowing that player to take you as close to the nest as you dare before attempting to tug him or her across it instead at the last moment.

Leapfrog

It is possible to play Leapfrog with just two players, but larger numbers will make for much more fun. Leapfrog can be played virtually anywhere, but soft grass is best.

How to Play

All the participants line up and "make a back" by placing their hands firmly on their thighs, with their feet apart for balance and their heads tucked down.

The person at the back of the line is the first Leaper. The Leaper takes a short run-up, puts his or her hands evenly on the first back, and leapfrogs over. He or she leaps over each player in the line, then runs forward a few paces and makes a back. At the same time, the person who is now at the end of the line begins leapfrogging.

The game continues until everyone has both leaped and been leapfrogged over.

When the first Leaper is back at the end of the line, he or she tries to jump over all the people in front again.

The aim is to keep the chain of leapfroggers going without everything turning into chaos.

The pressure is on for players to regain their balance and form a back quickly after leaping. This way they can avoid ending up on the ground when the next leapfrogger arrives.

Round and Round

Try Circle Leapfrog, with one person leaping around and around until he or she gives up and drops out.

You can be as inventive as you like with Leapfrog, so add as many variations as you wish.

Hopscotch

Hopscotch can be played anywhere that you can chalk out the classic layout. It can even be adapted to the pattern of the sidewalk near where you live.

How to Play

The most common layout used to play Hopscotch today is squares. Alternate between one square then two, finishing with a single square to make a total of ten.

Draw the layout of the Hopscotch pattern either by chalking it onto the ground or by marking it out in sand or dirt with a stick.

Number the squares from one to ten with your chalk or stick.

To start, throw a small pebble onto square 1. Make sure the pebble lands cleanly inside the box. If it lands touching a line, your turn is already over.

Jump over the square containing your pebble, landing with your left foot in square 2 and your right in 3. Continue, alternately hopping and jumping until you reach square 10. Then turn (balancing on one foot) to make your way back to your pebble. Stop on squares 2 and 3 to pick up the pebble before jumping over square 1 to complete the course.

If you touch a line with your foot, lose your balance, or miss a square, your turn is over.

Each time you successfully finish the course, throw your pebble to the next square in sequence. So your next throw would be into square 2. Hop through squares 1, 3, and 4.

Tactical Tips

It's best to find an odd-shaped stone, with a flat side that will not roll, and practice your throwing skills first.

Chinese Jump Rope

How to Play

Tie a length of thin elastic string about 9 feet long into a loop. Two Enders stand, facing each other, inside the loop and hold the elastic taut around their ankles. The third person must attempt to perform a sequence of jumps.

In a pinch you can stretch the elastic around the legs of two chairs and play solo if you want to practice by yourself.

Chant a rhyme while you jump to keep momentum:

> *England, Ireland, Scotland, Wales,*
> *Inside, outside, puppy dog tails!*

or

> *Jelly on a plate,*
> *Jelly on a plate,*
> *Wibble wobble, wibble wobble,*
> *Jelly on a plate.*

❧ Jump into the middle of the strings, facing one Ender.
❧ Jump so that each foot lands on a strand of elastic.
❧ Next, jump one foot in the middle, one outside the string.
❧ Turn and repeat before jumping into the middle again.
❧ Now jump so that your feet land on either side of the strings.
❧ Hook each string with your toes and cross your legs over.
❧ Release with a scissor kick, then land in the middle again.
❧ Jump out to one side, facing the string.
❧ Hooking the first string with your toes, jump across to the other side, making a diamond shape.
❧ Lastly, jump all the way out to one side in a graceful finish.

If successful, the Enders raise the elastic to knee level, then thighs, then waist, making each round more difficult. If you miss a jump, you're out, and one of the Enders takes a turn.

Double Dutch

These days, Double Dutch has become a competitive sport, but it's just as good with a couple of friends and some music. You'll need practice to get it right, but once you do, it's a lot of fun and excellent exercise, too.

How to Play

Double Dutch uses two long ropes swung in opposite directions (special Double Dutch ropes are available).

You'll need two Enders with arms strong enough to keep the ropes turning. This can be tricky at first, as it requires good coordination and some practice.

The Enders stand 6 to 9 feet apart, take a rope in each hand, and turn them alternately in large arcs. Their left hands should rotate the rope clockwise, and their right hands should rotate the rope counterclockwise.

Once a steady rhythm is established, it's time for the Skippers to jump in. They should stand beside one of the Enders and watch the ropes for a few moments, waiting for a window to open up between the ropes (when the nearest rope is on a downward swing) before trying to hop over it. They should then hop in on a diagonal and start jumping immediately!

Practice Makes Perfect

Start with simple two-footed jumps and skipping from foot to foot. Then practice turning around on the spot or hopping. Take turns so everyone has a chance to skip and turn the ropes.

Tactical Tip

Practice keeping a good rhythm going with a song or chant.

Pat-a-Cake

Pat-a-Cake is perfect to play in pairs, or several children can sit in a circle, clapping in time to a song.

How to Play

Face your partner, a little way apart, and clap hands in sequence, mirroring each other's actions.

- Clap your hands together, then clap both palms to your partner's palms.
- Clap hands, then clap your right hand to your partner's right hand, diagonally.
- Clap hands, then left hand to left hand, diagonally.
- Clap hands, then clap both palms to your partner's palms again.
- Repeat, with double claps.

When you've built up confidence, add in some extras:

- Clap both hands on your thighs.
- Clap your shoulders, knees, and toes.
- Bring your right hand down and your left hand up, clapping hands as your partner does the same.
- Reverse it!

Build up a rhythm to this classic by clapping rhymes.

> *A sailor went to sea, sea, sea,*
> *To see what he could see, see, see,*
> *But all that he could see, see, see,*
> *Was the bottom of the deep blue sea, sea, sea.*

Try to sing and clap faster and faster and continue for as long as possible without making any mistakes.

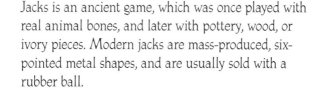

Jacks

Jacks is an ancient game, which was once played with real animal bones, and later with pottery, wood, or ivory pieces. Modern jacks are mass-produced, six-pointed metal shapes, and are usually sold with a rubber ball.

How to Play

You'll need a pack of ten jacks with a ball and someone to play against.

To start, throw the ball up in the air and pick up a jack from the ground with your throwing hand. Then try to catch the ball with the same hand before it bounces.

Repeat this move until you have picked up, and put aside, each jack once. This is known as Onesy.

Next try to pick up five groups of two jacks for Twosy, three groups of three and a single jack for Threesy, two groups of four and the remaining pair for Foursy, and finally, two groups of five for Fivesy.

When you miss, your opponent takes a turn.

If you are struggling, give yourself extra time to pick up the jacks by adding a bounce before you catch the ball.

Challenging Combinations

As you improve at Jacks, add challenging combinations, such as clapping while the ball is in the air before you scoop up any jacks.

Traditionally the last, and hardest, Jacks combination is called Everlastings. Throw all the jacks up into the air at once. Immediately turn your hand over and attempt to catch all of the jacks on the back of your hand.

Next, fling the jacks up from the back of your hand, picking up any that fell to the ground in the first place, before catching the rest safely in your palm. This takes some practice.

Tactical Tips

On the lower levels of a game of Jacks, throw the jacks so that they are scattered over a wide area. This makes it easier to pick up just one or two.

On higher levels, use a more gentle throw to keep the jacks closer together and make it easier to grab several at once.

Marbles

Marbles has been played all over the world for thousands of years in various forms.

Marble Technique

The usual technique of propelling a marble is known as Knuckling. Hook the marble in your index finger, with the knuckle resting on the ground. Then flick the marble with your thumb.

Lagging is a way of choosing who goes first: Each player rolls a marble toward an agreed target. The player whose marble is closest goes first.

Ring Marbles

A classic game of Ringy or Ring Taw Marbles is played in a circle, roughly 8 inches wide, marked out on flat ground. Each competitor places a marble in the ring. The players flick a marble toward the circle, aiming to knock out their opponent's marble. If successful, they can claim the marble. To keep things fair, it is a good idea to mark a second circle around the first as a shooting line.

Chasing and Hiding Games

There's nothing like a simple game of Tag or
Hide-and-Seek to while away long afternoons
and wear you out before dinner.

Tag

Nothing quite matches the simple spontaneity of a game of Tag in the playground or at a picnic.

How to Play

All you need to play is plenty of open space and several willing participants — at least five, but probably no more than twenty.

Use a decider from pages 8 to 13 to choose the chaser, usually known as It. Alternatively, everyone playing places his or her finger on his or her nose. The last person to do so is It.

All the players scatter, while It chases after them, trying to touch or tag someone by tapping him or her on the shoulder.

Anyone tagged instantly becomes It. There is a rule that anyone who is tagged cannot immediately tag back the person who got him or her — he or she must go after someone else. The game ends when the last person is caught, or as soon as dinner is ready.

The game itself has any number of versions as well as names — just a few are detailed on the following pages.

Chain Tag

Chain Tag requires good cooperation among the players for a successful chase. The smaller the space, the harder it is to escape from the chain!

How to Play

Begin the game as described on page 56, but when a player is tagged, he or she must hold hands with It and continue the chase together. As more players are tagged, the chain grows and grows, but a tag counts only if the whole chain is connected at the time of tagging.

If you get cornered, duck under the arms of two players in the chain and escape to freedom behind them.

The last person tagged wins the game.

In a speedier version of Chain Tag, players keep tagging until there are four people in the chain. The chain then splits into two pairs to chase down everyone else.

Tail Tag

A fun version of Tag for younger children, Tail Tag begins with all the players joined in a long "snake," one behind the other.

If there are more than seven or eight people, divide into two groups to play. The person at the front must lead everyone around, trying to tag the last person in the snake's tail. Once tagged, the person at the back becomes the leader.

Freeze Tag

Freeze Tag is an energetic game that challenges children's flexibility and balance as well as their speed. It's best played on the grass, as crawling on the ground is required.

How to Play

This is a variation on original Tag (see page 56). One person is chosen to be It, which means he or she must chase the other players and try to tag them. It runs up as close as possible to another player and uses either hand to reach out and touch that person.

The one touched must then stand still with legs and arms apart, as if they are frozen. Players who have not been tagged are able to free a frozen person simply by crawling between their legs.

Try to avoid being the last person unfrozen or you will become It for the next game.

Tactical Tip

If you are not It, help the other players to remain free
for as long as possible.

If you are It, try to tag all of the other players
as quickly as you can. Tag people who are
getting a little too close to freeing
frozen players first.

Crusts and Crumbs

This ancient chasing game is played with two teams, but begins without either side having any idea if it is doing the hunting or being hunted.

How to Play

You will need between six and twelve people to play. Divide into two teams and select one person to act as Caller (this is a good role for an adult to play, as the Caller does not take part in the game and can act as an umpire at the same time).

Traditionally, Crusts and Crumbs would have been played in the middle of the street, with the sidewalks on either side being the safe areas.

Playing in the park or at a playground is a more suitable alternative. Use bags and sweatshirts to mark out each end of a center line, with a safety line 12 to 15 feet away on either side.

The two teams line up to face each other about three feet apart at the center line, with one team as Crusts, the other as Crumbs.

When both teams are ready, the Caller shouts out "Crusts!" or "Crumbs!", either drawing out the beginning of the word to keep the suspense or yelling the word suddenly to surprise everyone.

Whichever team is called becomes the chasing team and must pursue the other team to their sidewalk or safe area.

Any player who is tagged switches to the opposing side until one team has caught all the members of the other team.

Twos and Threes

This is a tagging game that works well indoors, if space allows.

How to Play

You will need an even number of players, with six players as the absolute minimum. Start by getting into twos — one person behind the other — and stand in a circle with everyone facing the center.

Select one pair to go first, with the player on the outside being It and chasing the person in front.

If you are being chased, you are able to run wherever you like in and around the circle, and can escape tagging simply by stopping at the front of another pair, making a three.

At that moment, It has to leave you alone and begin chasing after the player at the back of the three.

Anyone tagged becomes It instead, and immediately starts to race after the person who tagged him or her.

Shadow Tag

A noncontact version of traditional Tag, Shadow Tag has one vital ingredient — sunshine.

Players are tagged if It can stand on their shadow, so it's best to play in the afternoon when shadows are longer. One key rule is that participants are not allowed to pause for any length of time in the shade.

Capture the Flag

This exhilarating strategy game can be played with many people over a large area. It's ideal if you happen to be on a picnic in a wooded area, but it works well on a soccer field or in a park, too. You need two flags on sticks, made from old T-shirts or any other spare pieces of fabric.

How to Play

Select two teams, and two territories, equal in size. This could simply be the two halves of a soccer field, or it may involve dividing up the area of the woods or field where you are playing.

Each team chooses a base where they will keep any prisoners. Then each team takes a flag and places it securely within their territory.

The aim is to capture your enemy's flag while defending your own. Teams can send individual members across or go in a big group, but if caught, players can be tagged and taken prisoner by the opposing team.

A team cannot capture the enemy flag until they have freed all their players by reaching the enemy base and tagging them.

Tactical Tips

It helps to think strategically when placing your flag. It must be difficult to reach (without being dangerous), and you will need to be able to see enemy players advancing in order to defend the spot well.

Hide-and-Seek

A simple game of Hide-and-Seek is perfect to play with smaller children and can be enjoyed indoors or out as long as the area of play is established before you start.

How to Play

The Hiders run off to find hiding spaces, while the Seeker counts to one hundred, possibly with hands over his or her eyes and facing a corner for good measure. When finished counting, the Seeker shouts, "Ready or not, here I come!" before setting off to find everyone.

The first player to be found is the next Seeker; the last person to be found is the winner of that game.

Sardines

Sardines is a fun variation on Hide-and-Seek, usually played indoors, unless there are the right kinds of hiding places available outside.

How to Play

Unlike traditional Hide-and-Seek, in Sardines one person goes off to hide, while all the other players count to one hundred, then split up to search. The key difference is that once a Seeker finds the Hider, they must join him or her in the hiding spot. The smaller the space chosen to hide, the more squashed up everyone will eventually be, until the last person discovers all the sardines.

Tactical Tip

Keep a close eye on your fellow Seekers. If a Seeker goes off to part of the house but doesn't return, there's a good chance that they have found the hiding place.

Block

(Kickstone One, Two, Three)

Block is an energetic variation on the classic Hide-and-Seek theme. The Seeker not only tries to find the Hiders, but has to race them back to the starting point, known as the block. The block, or "kickstone," was traditionally a lamppost, but it could just as easily be a street sign, tree, or stoop.

How to Play

The Seeker covers his or her eyes and counts to one hundred. The rest of the players scatter and hide. Then the hunting begins.

On spotting someone, the Seeker runs back to touch the block and shouts, "Block" or "Kickstone one, two, three, I spy [Name]," inserting the name of the person spotted. That person is then out, or "blocked."

For Hiders, the aim is to get back to the block before the Seeker, while shouting, "One, two, three, block home" or "Kickstone one, two, three."

The game continues until everyone is either home free or blocked. The person who was caught first becomes the Seeker for the next game.

Word and Memory Games

Give yourself a mental challenge with this selection
of the best mind-bending games ever.

I Spy

This is a classic game of observation that's perfect for filling time on a boring car trip or a long, hot summer afternoon. Can you spot something that no one else can?

How to Play

Choose someone to begin the game. Very often this is the person whose idea it was to play. The starting player secretly selects an object that everyone can see, before saying:

I spy with my little eye, something beginning with the letter [insert letter that the name of the object begins with].

The other players then look around for any possible objects beginning with that letter and take turns guessing what it is.

Logic is very important. If you are playing in a car, it's important that the object you pick is not left far behind you on the highway. For instance, don't pick *B* for *Bridge* unless you are stuck in a long line of traffic. Your chosen object will soon become a distant speck behind you. The first person to successfully guess the object gets to choose the next I Spy.

Tactical Tips

Consider the skill levels of your opponents. It's easier and quicker to pick something obvious, but spend a few moments planning ahead to make it as difficult as you can for the other players.

If you're playing against a particularly cunning opponent, keep an eye on their line of sight while they're choosing and while you guess the object.

Alphabet Minute

Alphabet Minute is played in teams of two, with as many pairs as you want. You'll just need paper and pencils for everyone, and a watch or clock to time people.

How to Play

Before the game starts, everyone writes down a simple topic of conversation on a slip of paper, such as the weather, or TV, along with a letter of the alphabet.

The papers are then folded and put into a hat or bowl.

The first team picks a paper and looks at the subject they have chosen and the letter of the alphabet specified. They must then strike up a conversation on that subject for sixty seconds.

The opening sentence has to begin with the specified letter, and subsequent sentences must begin with the following letters of the alphabet in sequence, until the speakers get back to the letter they began with or the sixty seconds is up.

Here's an example of how to get started:

Topic: TV
Letter: T

"The news is my favorite show on TV."
"Unbelievable, are you sure?"
"Vital to having great general knowledge, you know."
"Why? I'd rather play a game."
"X-ray research shows it's good for you."
"You're really strange."
"Zany is a better word."

After the letter Z, the game would continue with the letter A.

The winning team is the one who gets through the alphabet fastest, or who gets the furthest along in sixty seconds.

Fizz Buzz

This game is a great test of mental agility and an excellent way to pass the time on a long car trip.

It can just be a fun participation game, but you can add a competitive element by punishing mistakes with losses of "lives."

How to Play

Contestants must take turns counting from one to one hundred.

Each time you would usually say the number three, a number divisible by three, or a number that has a three in it, you must say, "Fizz" instead.

At the same time, whenever you would usually say the number seven, a number divisible by seven, or a number that has a seven in it, say, "Buzz" instead.

If a number is divisible by both three and seven or has a three and a seven in it, you must say, "Fizz Buzz."

For example:

"One, two, Fizz, four, five, Fizz, Buzz, eight, Fizz, ten, eleven, Fizz, Fizz, Buzz, Fizz, sixteen, Buzz, Fizz, nineteen, twenty, Fizz Buzz," and so on.

Any player who accidentally says a number rather than "Fizz," "Buzz," or "Fizz Buzz," uses up a life. Once everyone has taken a turn and reached one hundred, the player who has lost fewest lives is the winner.

Tactical Tip

For a simpler version use just "Fizz" for threes, or "Buzz" for sevens. This can easily be a game in itself, especially for younger players, or can be used to practice for the full knockout Fizz Buzz version.

I Went to Market

This is a fantastic game to sharpen your memory, and it's sure to make you laugh as you think up weirder items to buy. I Went to Market is perfect for younger players who are just learning the alphabet, or who are working to improve their memory skills.

How to Play

Players take turns suggesting the items bought at the market in alphabetical order by saying, "I went to market and I bought . . ." The first person begins with the letter *A* — "some apples," for example. Then the second person repeats "apples" before adding something of their own that begins with the letter *B*. The second person should say, "I went to market and bought some apples and some bread." The third player repeats the items beginning with *A* and *B* and adds another beginning with *C*, and so on. Agree beforehand if you think everyone should be allowed to pass over difficult letters like *X* and *Z*.

You can play the game with genuine market items such as apples and bread if you prefer, or use your imagination to buy anything and everything under the sun. If you get stuck on a particular letter, or you can't remember the complete sequence, you lose a life. If you lose three lives, you're out.

Kim's Game

Kim's Game is a great way to test your ability to recall details. The beauty of the game is that it's played with household objects, so it's just a question of using whatever you might have around the house.

How to Play

One person gathers together a selection of fifteen to twenty household objects and places them on a tray. Smaller items, such as a pen, a cotton ball, an apple, or a marble, are ideal.

Players have one minute to study and memorize the items before the tray is covered with a cloth.

All players have a piece of paper and a pen to write down as many of the items as they can remember. Each player scores a point for each item remembered correctly, but loses a point for any that were never there (it does happen!). The highest-scoring player wins.

You can play Kim's Game as a single round or over several rounds, allowing different players to set the challenge. With regular practice, players can increase the number of items they are able to remember.

Singing and Circle Games

A good sing-along is always popular, so gather around and
put your heart and voice into these childhood favorites.

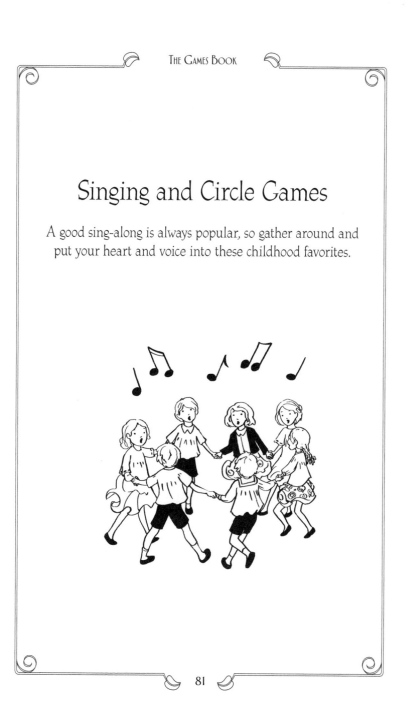

The Farmer in the Dell

This popular singing game is ideal for ten to twelve players, but more people can join in if space allows.

How to Play

Gather everyone into a circle. One player is chosen to be the Farmer. That player stands in the middle of the circle. The other players dance around the Farmer, singing:

The farmer in the dell,
The farmer in the dell,
Hi-ho the derry-o,
The farmer in the dell.

The farmer takes a wife,
The farmer takes a wife,
Hi-ho the derry-o,
The farmer takes a wife.

At this point the Farmer selects a "wife" from the circle. She goes to stand with him in the center, and everyone sings:

The wife takes a child,
The wife takes a child,
Hi-ho the derry-o,
The wife takes a child.

The child takes a nurse,
The child takes a nurse,
Hi-ho the derry-o,
The child takes a nurse.

The nurse takes a cow.
The nurse takes a cow.
Hi-ho the derry-o,
The nurse takes a cow.

The verses continue as the cow takes a dog, the dog takes a cat, the cat takes a rat, and the rat takes the cheese. On each verse, a person is selected to join the family in the center.

The Cheese is the last person chosen, and the final verse is:

The cheese stands alone,
The cheese stands alone,
Hi-ho the derry-o,
The cheese stands alone.

The Cheese then becomes the Farmer in the next round.

London Bridge Is Falling Down

How to Play

Two players make an arch while the other players dance, walk, or run through it singing the rhyme. At the end of the song, the players making the arch lower their arms and catch one of the other players.

> *London Bridge is falling down,*
> *Falling down, falling down,*
> *London Bridge is falling down,*
> *My fair lady.*
>
> *Take a key and lock her up,*
> *Lock her up, lock her up.*
> *Take a key and lock her up,*
> *My fair lady.*
>
> *We must build it up again,*
> *Up again, up again.*
> *We must build it up again,*
> *My fair lady.*
>
> *Build it up with gold and silver,*
> *Gold and silver, gold and silver.*
> *Build it up with gold and silver,*
> *My fair lady.*

Gold and silver I have none,
I have none, I have none.
Gold and silver I have none,
My fair lady.

Build it up with pins and needles,
Pins and needles, pins and needles.
Build it up with pins and needles,
My fair lady.

Pins and needles bend and break,
Bend and break, bend and break.
Pins and needles bend and break,
My fair lady.

Build it up with wood and clay,
Wood and clay, wood and clay.
Build it up with wood and clay,
My fair lady.

Wood and clay will wash away,
Wash away, wash away.
Wood and clay will wash away,
My fair lady.

Build it up with stone so strong,
Stone so strong, stone so strong.
Build it up with stone so strong,
My fair lady.

Stone so strong will last so long,
Last so long, last so long.
Stone so strong will last so long,
My fair lady.

In and Out the Dusty Bluebells

This is a great game for sunny days in the backyard or on the playground. You will need ten to twelve people.

How to Play

Everyone except It stands in a circle holding hands, raising their arms to make arches. It then skips around the circle, in and out of each arch, while everyone sings:

> In and out the dusty bluebells,
> In and out the dusty bluebells,
> In and out the dusty bluebells,
> Who shall be the leader?
>
> Tip tap, tip tap on your shoulder,
> Tip tap, tip tap on your shoulder,
> Tip tap, tip tap on your shoulder,
> You shall be the leader.

As the first verse finishes, It stops and taps the nearest player on the shoulder. The person tapped unlinks from the circle, grabs It around the waist from behind, and is led in and out of the arches while the song begins again. Each time the second verse is sung, another player is added to the back of the chain. For added emphasis, each player in the chain can tap the nearest person on the shoulder at the same time.

Knots

This game will get everyone tangled up in a knot. You'll need at least ten people for it to work well.

How to Play

With an even number of players standing in a circle, each person puts out a left hand and holds hands with another left hand. Everyone repeats with the right hand, but with a different person.

Now carefully unravel yourselves back into a circle. It's much harder than it sounds!

All Tangled Up

For a more chaotic version, everyone forms a line and holds hands with the people on both sides of them. The first in line dips between two arms, or crawls under someone's legs, bringing the whole line with them like a bizarre version of Follow the Leader.

Without letting go of one another's hands, everyone continues weaving in and out until they are all tied up in a huge knot. The last player in line has to untangle the knot without anyone letting go of their neighbors' hands.

Duck, Duck, Goose

This chasing game requires the ability to run quickly in a circle rather than in a straight line. The more people involved, the merrier, but the farther you'll have to run!

How to Play

Everyone sits in a large circle, facing inward. One person is selected as Goose and walks slowly around, touching each player gently on the head, saying "Duck" each time. When the time is right, the Goose touches the next person on the head and suddenly shouts, "Goose!"

That player must jump up and chase the Goose around the circle — be ready for a sprint! If the Goose gets around to the empty space before being tagged, the Goose becomes a Duck and sits down, and the loser becomes the new Goose.

Tactical Tip

Choose your tagged Duck wisely. Select someone who isn't paying much attention as you pass. Be ready to run as soon as you shout, "Goose!" to get a good head start on your opponent.

Ball Games

Ball games are the perfect combination of good fun, great exercise, and skill, and they're sure to exhaust even the most competitive child.

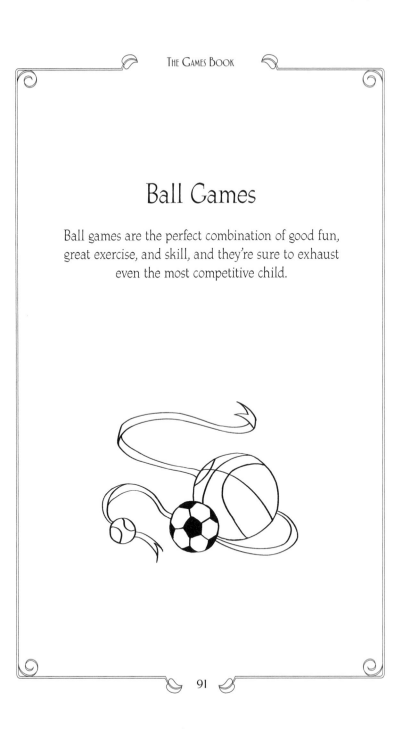

Queenie

This is a very simple game to play, as long as you can keep a straight face. It's at least a hundred years old and, despite the name, it's just as much fun for boys to play as it is for girls! It's best played with a small ball, such as a tennis ball, which will be easy to hide, and with a minimum of four or five players.

How to Play

Select one player to be Queenie and line up in a row behind her. Queenie tosses the ball over her shoulder without looking, and the other players immediately run after it. Once one player has the ball, everyone except Queenie lines up again with their hands behind their backs and chants:

> Queenie, Queenie, who's got the ball?
> I haven't got it; it isn't in my pocket,
> Queenie, Queenie, who's got the ball?

Queenie must then turn around and try to guess which player has the ball behind his or her back. If she guesses correctly, Queenie plays again, otherwise the person with the ball takes over.

Tactical Tip

If you do get the ball, remember not to give yourself away by crying out in excitement. It's also important to have a good poker face so that Queenie doesn't suspect you.

If you are Queenie, keep an eye out for giggling faces and shaking shoulders — they are sure to lead you straight to the person with the ball.

Kingy

This traditional ball game is a fast-paced, fun challenge for ten to fifteen players. Use a small, bouncy ball and play within a tennis court or playground so that it will be stopped by walls or fences if it goes astray.

How to Play

First choose a Chaser. If you suggested the game, this is a good excuse to elect yourself. Start by bouncing the ball ten times, giving the others a chance to spread out.

Get players out and onto your side by hitting them with the ball, aiming only between the shoulders and knees. You cannot run with the ball, but you can dribble it, bouncing it along the ground as you run to get close enough to aim.

Players who are hit correctly have to help you chase and throw, but once there are two or more people chasing, you are no longer allowed to move with the ball at all. Instead, you can throw the ball across to each other to cover more ground.

Defending players can ward off the ball by knocking it away with a clenched fist. However, if the ball is caught by a Chaser before it bounces, that player is out. The ball cannot be kicked or touched, other than with clenched fists, but gripping it between two fists to throw it out of the Chasers' reach is permitted. If players are tagged while holding the ball, they are also out.

The last player left is Kingy, and is allowed to decide who the next Chaser will be.

Bad Eggs

This popular game combines a good memory with running, ball-catching, and throwing skills.

How to Play

You'll need a tennis ball, an open space, and about six to eight players — any more makes it difficult to remember everyone's identity. Choose a category such as colors, days of the week (as long as the number of players is not more than seven), or numbers. Assign a color, day, or number to each player.

One player starts with the ball and throws it up in the air, calling out one of the colors or days of the week at the same time. If your color is called, you must run in to catch the ball, while everyone else tries to get as far away as possible.

When the ball is caught, shout "Stop!" to make everyone freeze. Take three giant strides toward another player, and throw the ball, attempting to hit that player below the knees. A hit gives that player one Bad Egg, or penalty point, for the next round. If you throw and miss, you get the Bad Egg.

Three Bad Eggs and you're out.
Someone else then gets the ball to
start the game again.

Tactical Tip

Sometimes rolling the ball along the
ground can be easier and more
accurate than throwing it.

Sevens

You can play this ball game alone or with friends. The difficulty increases the further you progress, and it can take hours to complete and years to perfect.

How to Play

Find a tennis ball and a flat outside wall. Stand about six feet from the wall and follow the directions for each stage below:

- Throw the ball at the wall and catch it.
- Hit the wall, let it bounce, catch it.
- Hit the wall, swat the ball back with the palm of your hand, and catch it.
- Hit the wall, swat it back at the wall, let it bounce once, and catch it.
- Hit the wall, let it bounce once, bounce it again with the palm of your hand, and catch it.

- Hit the wall, swat it back at the wall, let it bounce once, bounce it again with your hand, and catch it.
- Hit the wall, swat it back at the wall, let it bounce, bounce it again, swat it back at the wall, and catch it.

When you have mastered these moves, begin again, adding the following variations on each maneuver:

- Clap your hands each time you throw the ball.
- Clap your hands twice after throwing the ball.
- Spin around each time you throw the ball.
- Go through each stage using only your right hand.
- Go through each stage using only your left hand.
- Start each stage by throwing the ball under your right leg.
- Start each stage by throwing the ball under your left leg.

If all that is too easy, you can combine as many skill variations as you like. Then challenge a friend to a Sevens championship match!

String, Card, and Paper Games

You only need a few basic supplies to play a dozen different fun and absorbing rainy-day games.

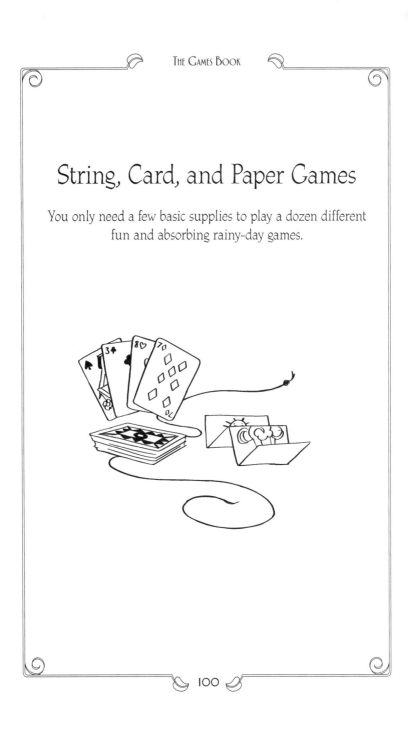

Cat's Cradle

This string game for two players will keep you occupied for hours on end.

How to Play

1

Tie a 64-inch piece of string into a loop. Then put both hands, except the thumbs, inside the loop and wrap it around each hand again. With your middle finger, hook the string that lies across the opposite palm from underneath and pull. Repeat with the other hand to make Cat's Cradle (1).

Soldier's Bed

2

Using both thumbs and index fingers, your partner should pinch the Cat's Cradle from above at the two points where the strings crisscross (2) and then pull the crosses

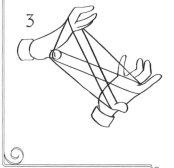

3

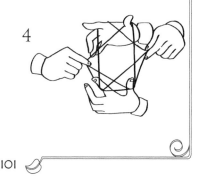

4

around the outside strings and scoop them up through the center. Let the Cradle go so that your partner can pull it taut (3).

Candles

In exactly the same way, grip the two points on the Soldier's Bed where the long strings intersect (4). Scoop them around and up through the center. As you draw the strings apart, they will form four parallel lines (5).

Manger

Using both little fingers, your partner now hooks the inside string next to your index finger and the inside string next to your thumb, pulling them out to make a square (6). Your partner then scoops up the outside strings with both thumbs and index fingers, making a reverse Cradle (7).

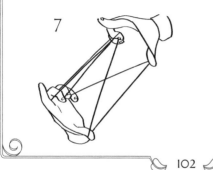

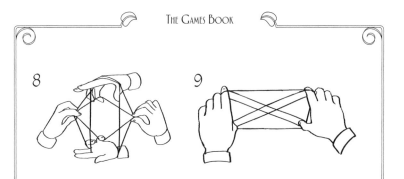

Diamonds

In the same way your partner made the Soldier's Bed, bring the crosses around the outside strings (8), but instead go down into the center before pulling taut (9).

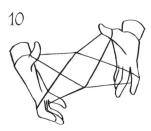

Cat's Eyes

Your partner then repeats the actions you used to make Candles, but a pattern of four triangles is mysteriously created instead (10).

Fish in a Dish

Now put your thumbs and index fingers down into each of the triangles, scoop up through the center, and pull out to make your Fish in a Dish (11).

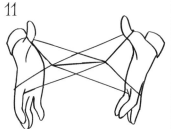

Snap

Perfect for beginners, Snap is a great game for kids. Quick reflexes are essential. But remember: Shouting loudest doesn't mean you're first!

How to Play

Snap can be played with just two players, or with several. Use an extra pack of cards if more than four people are playing.

Deal the cards out among players as evenly as possible. Players should keep their cards piled facedown in front of them. The player on the dealer's left begins, turning his or her top card faceup and creating a new central stack.

Players take turns placing a card on the central stack, keeping watch for a card with a matching number underneath it. When this happens, the first to shout "Snap!" takes all the cards in the central pile and adds them to the bottom of his or her stack.

The next player to the left continues the game. Players are out of the game when their stack runs out. The Snap champion is the player who wins all the cards in play.

Slapjack

This card game is fast, furious, and a great kids' favorite that's ideal for two to four players.

How to Play

The dealer shuffles the pack, then deals all fifty-two cards in a clockwise direction, starting with the player to the dealer's left.

Players hold their cards facedown in the palm of one hand, but do not look at them. The person to the left of the dealer begins, turning up his or her topmost card and placing it in the center. Play continues in dealing order.

Everyone watches carefully for a jack to appear and tries to be the first to slap a hand over the jack to win the cards in the center pile. Those cards are then added to the bottom of the pile in the winning player's hand, and the game continues with the next player to the left.

Players who lose all their cards to the other players can still stay in the game. They should count the jacks and, after three have appeared, pay extra attention to make sure they are the first to Slapjack. When one player has all the cards, the game is over.

Solitaire

This is an excellent solo card game that's great on a long Sunday.

How to Play

Shuffle a pack of cards, then deal seven cards facedown in a row. Deal a second card on each pile except the first, then a third card on each pile except the first two and so on, until the seventh pile has seven cards. This row forms your main Solitaire layout. Turn the top card of each pile over and keep the remaining cards facedown in a single stack.

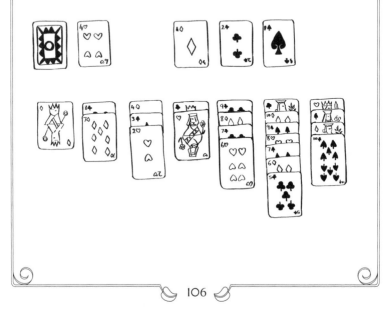

Cards on the main layout can be moved to sit below the next highest card of the opposite color. When a card has been moved, turn over the facedown card just uncovered.

Build up runs of cards on the main layout in alternating color order from high to low values. When you come across aces, start four individual "foundation" piles above the main layout. Your goal is to add cards of the same suit in ascending order from ace to king to these foundation piles as they are revealed in the main layout.

If you find you cannot move any cards, use the stack of spare cards to help move the game along. Turn over each card in the pile one by one, and if you can place it in one of the columns, do so. If you cannot, discard it in a faceup pile, keeping the topmost card free to play.

When one of the seven columns becomes empty, you can move a king, or a run starting with a king, into the gap.

Tactical Tip

It's important not to move cards to the foundation piles too soon as, once there, they cannot be moved. You may need certain cards later to allow the game to continue.

Clock Solitaire

This is a classic Solitaire game played in a circular pattern.

How to Play

Deal twelve cards facedown in a pattern that mimics the numbers on a clock face with another card in the center of your "clock." Repeat until you have four cards in each pile.

To start, turn over the top card on the center pile. This directs you to one of the piles on the clock face. Aces are at one o'clock, twos are at two o'clock, all the way around to queens at twelve o'clock.

Place your card under the pile or beside it. Turn over the top card of this pile to find out where to go next.

Whenever you turn over a king, you must place it in the center and take a card from the center pile to start again. The goal is to turn over all the cards in the twelve piles. However, once you have revealed all four kings, the game is over.

Rummy

Rummy makes for a perfect family game, as children can easily compete against adults.

How to Play

For two players, deal ten cards each. Three to four players get seven cards each, and five to six have six cards each. The rest of the pack is placed in a facedown stack, and the top card is turned faceup next to it.

The object of the game is to be the first player to get rid of all your cards. Cards can be discarded if they can be grouped into "books" — three or four of a kind — or "runs" — three or more cards of the same suit in order (note that aces are low).

When players look at their hands, they should start to organize the cards into these groups.

Play Begins

The person to the left of the dealer begins, choosing to pick up either the faceup card in the center or the unknown card from the top of the stack. They must

then place one unwanted card from their hand faceup on the discard pile.

If the player can already make a run or book, now is the time to lay it down, faceup on the table, before the next person takes their turn.

If any players hold cards that match a book or run that has been placed on the table, they can lay these cards down when it's their turn.

The winner of the round is the first to lay down all their cards. The values of the remaining cards are added up to make the winner's score. Kings, queens, and jacks count for ten points, aces one point; the remaining cards are valued as the number on the card.

Play continues until one player reaches one hundred points and wins the whole game.

Tactical Tips

Try to avoid taking cards from the discard pile, as this will let other players know the cards you are looking for.

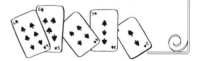

Beetle

A simple dice game for two or more people, players must compete to complete their beetle first.

How to Play

Each person has paper and a pencil. Players take turns rolling the dice, and the person scoring the highest number starts the game. Play then moves in a clockwise direction. Everyone must roll a six before they are allowed to draw the beetle's head. Only then can they draw the rest of the beetle, although the other body parts can be added in any order. Roll:

- One for each of the Beetle's two wings.
- Two for its tail.
- Three for each of its antennae.
- Four for each of the two eyes.
- Five for each of the six legs.
- Six for the Beetle's head.

As soon as your beetle is done, shout, "Beetle!" to stop the game and claim victory.

Consequences

This makes an excellent game for rainy days and quiet evenings. As many as eight people can play — you'll just need enough paper and pencils for everyone.

How to Play

Each person writes down the name of a boy, then folds his or her piece of paper over before passing it to the left. On the next line everyone writes:

met [inserting the name of a girl]
and folds and passes the paper along.
Each player then adds:
in/at [the name of a place].
Then everyone describes the clothes the girl was wearing.
The next person must write down the clothes that the boy was wearing, then:
He [each person writes down what the boy did].
Then she [everyone should describe what the girl did] before switching to write:
He said . . .
Then: *she said . . .* and finally:
The consequences were . . .

When the paper is unfolded, it might read:

*Jack met Carrie at the roller rink. Carrie was wearing pink
jeans and a green cardigan with sequins. Jack was wearing his
school uniform. He got hiccups. Then she did a cartwheel. He
said, "There's a fly in my soup." She said, "Where did you get
that hat?" The consequences were that the rain ruined the
barbecue.*

Each time you write a line of the story, you'll be completely
unaware of the previous element, so the consequences can
be quite bizarre. Your stories will be even funnier if the
characters involved are people that you all know, or if they
are well-known celebrities.

Picture Perfect

As an alternative, try Picture Perfect. The object of the game is
to collectively draw a person, with the funniest results possible.
Paper and pencils, plus markers if you like, are the only
equipment necessary.

How to Play

Divide the paper into several sections depending on the
number of players. First draw a head and neck, then fold
the paper over so that it can't be seen except for the bottom
of the neck. This will indicate to the next player where he or

she should continue. That player then draws the chest, shoulders, and arms, and folds the paper over before handing it on. The next player draws the whole lower part of the body, down to the knees. Finally, the last player draws the lower legs, feet, and shoes.

Tactical Tips

The more gruesome and exaggerated the features and clothing you draw, the funnier it will be. Once you've all got the hang of it, you can suggest titles for your pictures, such as "The man you'll marry" or "What our history teacher looks like."

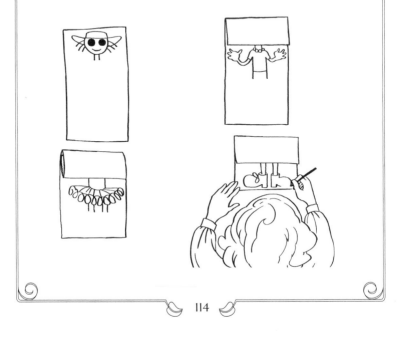

Hangman

A reliable favorite for a quiet afternoon indoors, Hangman is a classic word game for two or more players. You'll need to guess your opponent's word before the gallows is built and the "prisoner" is hanged!

How to Play

Think of a word and mark down on a piece of paper dashes for the number of letters it has. The other player must guess the word by suggesting letters. If the other player guesses a letter correctly, write it on the appropriate dash.

Each time the guess is wrong, add another piece of the gallows! Start with the base, then a vertical strut, a diagonal crosspiece, the horizontal arm, a diagonal section to hold it up, followed by the rope.

There are six more chances for your opponent to figure out the word — the head, body, two arms, and two legs of a hanging man.

Tactical Tip

Certain letters of the alphabet occur more often than others, so guess the most common letters first: *E, S, A,* and *T.*

Tic-tac-toe

Possibly the simplest tactical game ever, Tic-tac-toe is still a highly competitive way to keep busy.

How to Play

Draw a grid of four intersecting lines (two vertical, two horizontal) to make nine small squares. Choose Xs or Os, then toss a coin to see who will start.

Your aim is to get three Xs or three Os in a line, horizontally, vertically, or diagonally. To start, draw your X or O in any one of the nine spaces. Your opponent then draws in the opposite letter, concentrating on how to block your next move as well as trying to start a new row.

Nine Men's Morris

Nine Men's Morris is an ancient board game for two people.
It can easily be played using paper and pencil to draw a board
with coins serving as the Men.

How to Play

Draw three concentric squares and mark the corners and
halfway points of each with a dot. Link the halfway points with
vertical and horizontal lines.

Gather nine Men each, whether they are bottle caps, buttons,
pebbles, or coins, as long as they differ from your opponent's.
Decide who will start and take turns placing your Men on
empty dots on the board.

Once all the pieces are on the board, take turns moving them
to adjacent points, aiming to line up three Men, either
horizontally or vertically, in a row called a mill.

Each time you are successful, you can remove any one of your
opponent's Men from the board, as long as it is not already
part of a mill.

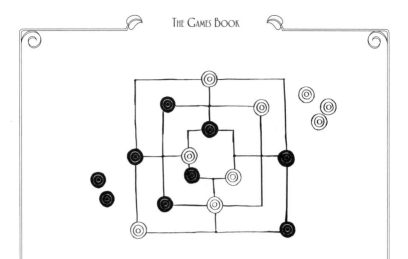

If your opponent moves two Men into a line, try to get to a blocking position to prevent your opponent from adding a third.

When your opponent is unable to move any of his or her Men or has only two pieces left, you are the winner.

An extra rule in some versions allows players to move pieces anywhere on the board, regardless of lines, if they are reduced to just three Men. Decide whether to play by this rule before the game begins.

Tactical Tip

Try to set up two safe mills, which your opponent cannot reach. Switch between the two to keep making mills, reducing your opponent's Men.

If you liked **The Games Book**, you'll
love **The Nursery Rhyme Book**!

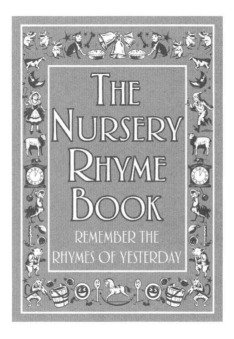

Turn the page for a sneak peek!

Peter, Peter, Pumpkin Eater

Peter, Peter, pumpkin eater,
Had a wife and couldn't keep her;
He put her in a pumpkin shell,
And there he kept her very well.

Peter, Peter, pumpkin eater,
Had another and didn't love her;
Peter learned to read and spell,
And then he loved her very well.

Mary, Mary, Quite Contrary

Mary, Mary, quite contrary,
How does your garden grow?
With silver bells and cockleshells,
And pretty maids all in a row.

Bobby Shafto

Bobby Shafto's gone to sea,
Silver buckles on his knee;
He'll come back and marry me,
Bonny Bobby Shafto!

Bobby Shafto's fat and fair,
Combing down his yellow hair;
He's my love forevermore,
Bonny Bobby Shafto!

Lucy Locket

Lucy Locket lost her pocket,
Kitty Fisher found it;
Not a penny was there in it,
Only ribbon 'round it.

Rain, Rain, Go Away

Rain, rain, go away,
Come again another day.

Rain, rain, go to Spain,
Never show your face again!

Humpty Dumpty

Humpty Dumpty sat on a wall,
Humpty Dumpty had a great fall.
All the king's horses,
And all the king's men,
Couldn't put Humpty together again.